Colophon

©Mathias Jansson (2025)

" Artificial Imagination: Artists and AI from the 1960s to Today"

ISBN: 978-91-86915-82-7

Published by:

 "jag behöver inget förlag"

c/o Mathias Jansson

Tvärvägen 23

232 52 Åkarp

SWEDEN

http://mathiasjansson72.blogspot.se/

Print: Lulu.com

Disclaimer: This book is written with help of ChatGPT. The author has previously conducted extensive research on the subject and has also contributed with texts about AI in books and journals. The essays have been improved, edited and proofread by the author before publishing.

Contents

Introduction: Art in the Age of Artificial Intelligence 3

Chapter 1 – What is Artificial Intelligence? 5

Chapter 2 – The First Encounters 9

Chapter 3 – Artists as Programmers 13

Chapter 4 – The Age of Machine Learning 17

Chapter 5 – AI Art Goes Mainstream 26

Chapter 6: Text-to-Image Revolution 31

Chapter 7: AI and Contemporary Art Today 35

Chapter 8 – Promptography: Images Without a Camera 41

Chapter 9 – Art Museums in the Age of AI 46

Chapter 10 – Futures of AI and Art 50

Chapter 11: Toward Posthuman Creativity 54

Glossary of Key Terms 58

Introduction: Art in the Age of Artificial Intelligence

For as long as humans have built machines, we have imagined what it would mean if they could think, speak, or even create like us. From the ancient myth of Pygmalion's living statue to Mary Shelley's *Frankenstein*, the dream of artificial creativity has haunted human culture. At the heart of this dream lies a persistent wish: to invent a machine that not only calculates but also creates—a partner in the most human of activities, imagination.

Artificial Intelligence (AI) has come closer than any previous technology to fulfilling that wish. What began as speculative mathematics in the 1940s and 1950s has evolved into systems capable of writing poetry, generating images, composing music, and improvising alongside humans. The arrival of machine learning and neural networks has transformed AI into something both powerful and mysterious—an engine of creativity that unsettles our old definitions of art, authorship, and originality.

Artists have always been at the front lines of experimenting with new tools, and AI is no exception. From the earliest algorithmic drawings in the 1960s to today's immersive installations, AI has not simply been used to make images but to ask critical questions: Who owns creativity in a world of automated systems? Can a dataset be considered a palette? What happens when algorithms reproduce the biases of the society that created them?

This book is a journey through that intersection of AI and contemporary art. It traces how artists have embraced, challenged, and reimagined artificial intelligence across six decades of practice. Along the way, we will encounter pioneers like Harold Cohen, who taught his program *AARON* to paint; contemporary figures like Mario Klingemann and Refik Anadol, who use neural networks as artistic collaborators; and critical voices like Trevor Paglen and Hito Steyerl, who expose the hidden politics of algorithmic vision.

AI in art is not just about dazzling new images or futuristic machines—it is about rethinking what creativity means when it is shared with non-human agents. It is about asking how culture is shaped when algorithms become part of our everyday tools. Most of all, it is about recognizing that our age-old desire to build a creative machine is not merely a technological challenge but a profoundly artistic one.

This book does not claim to answer all the questions AI poses to art. Instead, it offers a map: a way of tracing the history, practices, tools, and debates that define AI as a medium of contemporary art. From playful experiments to urgent critiques, the works we will explore remind us that art's role is not to celebrate technology uncritically, but to question, to reveal, and to imagine other possible futures.

Chapter 1 – What is Artificial Intelligence?

Artificial Intelligence (AI) is a term that often conjures futuristic images of robots, thinking machines, or vast data systems. But at its core, AI refers to the attempt to design machines that can perform tasks usually associated with human intelligence: learning, reasoning, problem-solving, understanding language, and, increasingly, creating. While scientists and engineers have given many technical definitions of AI, what interests us here is not only the mathematics of algorithms but the cultural imagination that surrounds them—the belief that machines might think or even create.

The First Dream: Ada Lovelace and the Creative Machine

The idea of a creative machine is older than the computer itself. In the 1840s, Ada Lovelace, often called the world's first programmer, wrote about Charles Babbage's Analytical Engine—a mechanical computer that was never built but conceptually groundbreaking. Lovelace suggested that such a machine might one day compose elaborate and scientific pieces of music of any degree of complexity or extent.

This statement was remarkable: while her contemporaries saw machines mainly as number-crunchers, Lovelace imagined them as potential artists. She understood that creativity itself might be translated into rules and operations, and that machines could perhaps take part in what had always been considered the most human of activities: art. Many scholars today regard her vision as a precursor to the field of creative AI, where the goal is not just to automate logic but to generate novelty, beauty, and expression.

The Birth of Artificial Intelligence

The term "Artificial Intelligence" was first used in 1956 at the Dartmouth Conference, a meeting that brought together pioneers such as John McCarthy, Marvin Minsky, and Claude Shannon. Their ambition was bold: to create machines that could replicate every aspect of human intelligence. Early projects attempted to simulate reasoning, problem-solving, and even conversation. Alan Turing had already proposed his famous "Imitation Game" (later known as the Turing Test) as a way of measuring whether a machine could convincingly mimic human thought.

But from the beginning, there was a tension between rational AI (machines that solve problems) and creative AI (machines that make new things). While engineers worked on logic and calculation, artists and visionaries were fascinated by the possibility of a machine that might paint, compose music, or tell stories.

AI as Metaphor and Medium

AI is not just a technical invention—it is also a powerful metaphor. It embodies our hopes and fears about intelligence, agency, and the role of technology in society. This dual identity has made it particularly attractive to artists, who often use AI as both a tool and a subject of critique. When an artist works with an algorithm, the result is not simply an image or sound but also a statement about the nature of creativity, authorship, and human-machine relations.

From Rules to Learning

In its early decades, AI was dominated by rule-based systems: programs that followed step-by-step instructions to simulate reasoning. But in the late 20th and early 21st century, the field shifted to machine learning, where computers "learn" patterns from large datasets rather than following pre-set rules. This shift was crucial for art: instead of telling the machine exactly how to draw, compose, or write, artists could feed it data—images, texts, sounds—and let the machine discover patterns and generate new forms.

This transition from programming rules to training models is what allowed AI to move beyond the laboratory into the hands of artists. It is the difference between Lovelace's dream of a machine that could follow instructions to make music, and today's systems like GPT or Stable Diffusion, which can generate music, text, or images that surprise even their creators.

Why AI Matters for Contemporary Art

For artists, AI is not just another tool like a brush or a camera. It is a collaborator, a critic, and a mirror. It forces us to ask: if a machine can paint a picture or write a poem, what does that mean for our understanding of creativity? Is art defined by the maker's intent, by the process, or by the experience of the audience?

This chapter has sketched the origins of AI, from Lovelace's prophetic vision to the rise of machine learning. In the following chapters, we will see how artists across decades have explored these questions—not to provide final answers, but to use AI as a way of expanding what art can be.

Chapter 2 – The First Encounters

When computers first entered the cultural landscape in the 1960s, they were seen as machines of calculation, not creation. They filled entire rooms, required specialized knowledge to operate, and were designed primarily for science, government, and the military. Yet even at this early stage, artists saw in them something more: the possibility of a new medium. By writing algorithms—sets of instructions for the machine to follow—artists began to explore whether creativity itself could be encoded into processes and rules. These first encounters with computer art set the foundation for today's AI practices.

Algorithmic Art and the Logic of Creativity

One of the earliest pioneers was Vera Molnar, a Hungarian-born French artist who began working with computers in the late 1960s. Molnar had already been experimenting with systematic drawings using a set of "imaginary machines" before gaining access to an actual computer. When she finally did, she created geometric compositions where slight variations in the algorithm introduced unpredictability and play. Her work suggested that creativity could be found not only in spontaneous gestures but also in the controlled mutations of a system.

Another key figure was Frieder Nake, a German mathematician and artist, who produced plotter drawings by programming computers to generate abstract forms. His works emphasized the tension between human authorship and machine execution: the artist wrote the code, but the machine produced the drawing. This tension remains central in today's AI art debates.

Harold Cohen and *AARON*

Perhaps the most famous example of early computer art is Harold Cohen's AARON. Beginning in the early 1970s, Cohen, a British painter, developed a computer program that could generate drawings autonomously. Over decades, he refined AARON into a system capable of producing increasingly complex, colorful, and recognizable imagery. Cohen described AARON not as a tool but as a collaborator—an independent entity with its own style and limitations.

AARON anticipated many of the questions that still occupy AI art today: Can a machine have a "style"? Who is the true author of a work—the programmer, the system, or both? And can we consider the output of a program "art" if it lacks human intention in the moment of creation?

Cybernetics and Interactive Systems

While some artists focused on algorithmic image-making, others were fascinated by cybernetics—the study of feedback systems between humans and machines. Nam June Paik, a pioneer of video art, collaborated with the cybernetician Shuya Abe to build interactive works that responded to viewers in real time. His installations anticipated today's AI-driven interactive art, where machines sense, process, and react to human presence.

Cybernetics inspired artists to imagine art as a dialogue between human and machine rather than a one-way expression. This relational approach foreshadowed later AI artworks where the system adapts, improvises, or learns from interaction with audiences.

Artificial Life and Early Experiments in Learning

By the late 1970s and 1980s, researchers and artists alike began exploring the idea of artificial life: systems that could evolve or adapt like living organisms. Simple learning algorithms and evolutionary art experiments hinted that machines might not just follow rules but also change over time. Artists like Manfred Mohr explored how randomness and variation could be introduced into algorithmic works, giving rise to unpredictable outcomes.

Although these early systems were far simpler than today's deep learning models, they planted the seed of a new artistic approach: one where machines were not only tools but also dynamic partners in creation.

Why These Experiments Still Matter

Looking back, the computer art of the 1960s–1980s may seem primitive compared to today's AI-generated images and texts. Yet these works established key artistic strategies that remain vital:

- Treating algorithms as a medium for creativity.
- Exploring the tension between human intention and machine autonomy.
- Using machines not only to produce forms but to question what art and authorship mean.

When Vera Molnar introduced randomness into her algorithmic drawings, or when Harold Cohen let AARON "decide" how to draw, they were not simply experimenting with new technology. They were probing the deeper cultural desire that Ada Lovelace had already identified: the wish to create a machine capable of original, creative acts.

These first encounters remind us that AI art did not appear suddenly in the 2010s—it is part of a long lineage of artists challenging the boundaries of art, creativity, and technology.

Chapter 3 – Artists as Programmers

By the late 1980s, computers had become more accessible, and artists no longer had to rely solely on research labs to gain access to technology. Personal computers, early graphic software, and programming languages opened new possibilities. Artists began to see the computer not just as a tool but as a medium in its own right. This period marked the emergence of artists as programmers, where writing code was itself considered an artistic act.

The 1980s and 1990s were also a time when computer science experimented with artificial life, evolutionary systems, and neural networks. These ideas filtered into art, giving rise to works that blurred the boundary between science and aesthetics.

From Algorithms to Evolutionary Art

A central figure of this era is Karl Sims, who became known for his pioneering experiments with evolutionary art. Sims created programs where virtual organisms—shapes, forms, or even simulated creatures—were subject to a kind of digital natural selection. Their survival depended on their ability to move, adapt, or evolve according to programmed conditions.

His famous work *Evolved Virtual Creatures* (1994) presented strange, computer-generated lifeforms that learned how to walk, swim, or fight. Though grounded in biology and computer science, the work resonated as art because it suggested machines could evolve creativity through processes beyond direct human control. The results were not designed in detail by Sims but emerged from the interaction between algorithm and system.

This kind of "bottom-up" creativity was a major departure from the rule-based approaches of the 1960s and 1970s. Instead of telling the machine exactly what to do, artists created environments where forms could grow, mutate, and surprise both their creators and audiences.

Generative and Interactive Art

Other artists explored how code could generate infinite variations of artworks. Manfred Mohr, who had begun with algorithmic drawings in the 1970s, expanded his practice in the 1980s and 1990s to include generative systems that continuously produced new compositions. His art emphasized process over final form, foregrounding the computer's ability to produce endless permutations.

At the same time, the rise of interactivity opened a new dimension. Artists such as Jeffrey Shaw developed immersive installations where audiences could navigate virtual spaces in real time. These works suggested that creativity could emerge from the interaction between humans and machines, with the artwork evolving according to user choices.

Neural Networks and Early AI Experiments

Although the neural networks of the 1980s and 1990s were relatively simple compared to today's deep learning, they fascinated artists as models of machine "thought." Some artists began experimenting with pattern recognition, computer vision, and rudimentary adaptive systems. These early steps were less about creating polished artworks and more about testing the boundaries of what machines could "see" or "learn."

Software Art and Net Art

By the 1990s, the rise of the internet and the increasing accessibility of programming sparked a new generation of software art and net art. Artists like Jodi (Joan Heemskerk and Dirk Paesmans) manipulated code, glitches, and the aesthetics of the web to challenge ideas of authorship and interaction. While not AI in the strict sense, this movement shared with AI art an interest in systems, algorithms, and machine-mediated creativity.

The net art movement also introduced performance into digital practice. Interventions in online spaces, sometimes humorous, sometimes critical, blurred the line between human and machine agency—a theme that would become central in later AI-based performances.

Why This Period Matters

The 1980s and 1990s represent a transitional moment: from algorithmic pioneers who used mainframes in the 1960s and 1970s, to a more diverse scene where artists coded their own systems, engaged with ideas of evolution and artificial life, and explored interactivity on personal computers and the internet.

The central artistic question shifted: from *"Can a computer produce art?"* to *"What happens when an artist writes the rules and lets the system create?"* This logic of generativity, emergence, and interaction still underpins much of contemporary AI art today, where artists often build systems that can surprise them, rather than control every outcome.

Chapter 4 – The Age of Machine Learning

The early 2000s marked a decisive turning point in the relationship between artificial intelligence and art. While artists in the 1980s and 1990s had experimented with evolutionary systems, rule-based algorithms, and interactivity, the rise of machine learning introduced an entirely new paradigm: instead of writing every rule by hand, artists could train systems to *learn* patterns from data.

This shift—from programming logic to training models—opened up vast new possibilities for creative practice. It also brought fresh ethical and cultural questions, as artists realized that data itself carries histories, biases, and power structures.

The Dataset as Palette

Machine learning works by exposing algorithms to large collections of data: images, sounds, texts. The system "learns" by identifying patterns in this material and then generating new variations. For artists, this meant that datasets became a kind of palette or material. By curating the data, artists could shape what the machine would learn to "see" or "imagine."

Anna Ridler's *Mosaic Virus* (2018)

One of the clearest demonstrations of how artists treat datasets as cultural material is Anna Ridler's *Mosaic Virus* (2018). The work consists of an AI-generated animation of tulips, continuously blooming and withering in shifting forms. At first glance, the piece might seem like a simple generative artwork—a computer producing endless variations of flowers. But beneath its surface lies a carefully constructed connection between biology, history, and economics.

To create the project, Ridler did not simply download an existing dataset from the internet, as is common in machine learning. Instead, she painstakingly built her own. She photographed thousands of tulips by hand and annotated them with detailed labels, creating a dataset that was personal, curated, and specific. By doing so, she positioned herself not only as the "artist" but also as the gardener of data, reminding us that datasets are not neutral—they are cultivated, selected, and framed by human choices.

The title *Mosaic Virus* refers to a real virus that infected tulips in the 17th century, causing their petals to break into spectacular streaks of color. These infected flowers became highly prized during the Dutch "tulip mania," one of the first recorded financial bubbles in history. Prices skyrocketed before crashing, ruining many who had speculated on the bulbs' value.

Ridler connects this historical episode to contemporary financial speculation by linking the blooming of her AI tulips to fluctuations in the price of Bitcoin. As cryptocurrency values rise and fall, the flowers in *Mosaic Virus* shift in form, creating a direct visual metaphor between the volatility of financial markets and the fragile beauty of tulips.

Memo Akten and Human–Machine Collaboration

Turkish artist Memo Akten became one of the most visible figures in this new wave of AI art. His projects often combined deep learning with performance, exploring the poetic and spiritual dimensions of machine creativity. In works like *Learning to See* (2017), Akten trained neural networks on specific visual materials (like flowers or clouds) and then had the system interpret live webcam footage through those datasets. The result was an uncanny experience where reality appeared transformed by the "eyes" of the machine.

For Akten, the artwork was not only the images produced but also the process of making visible how machines perceive the world—raising questions about perception, mediation, and meaning.

Mario Klingemann and *Memories of Passersby I* (2018)

Among the artists who helped define AI as a medium in contemporary art, Mario Klingemann holds a special place. Based in Germany, Klingemann was one of the earliest to experiment with Generative Adversarial Networks (GANs) not as a technical curiosity but as an aesthetic and conceptual tool. His practice explores how machines "see" and "imagine," often producing results that hover between recognition and abstraction, beauty and distortion.

Klingemann describes himself not simply as an artist but as a kind of "machine wrangler," someone who coaxes algorithms into revealing unexpected forms. He is interested in how networks trained on vast datasets internalize cultural patterns and then remix them into uncanny variations. The results are often portraits, figures, or landscapes that seem familiar yet unsettlingly alien—what he calls "the uncanny valley of the mind."

One of his most significant works is *Memories of Passersby I* (2018), a self-contained installation that consists of a wooden cabinet housing a pair of computer screens and a neural network running live on a computer inside. Instead of showing a fixed set of images, the system continuously generates an endless flow of portraits, each unique and ephemeral, appearing for only a brief moment before dissolving into the next.

The portraits seem painterly, reminiscent of 18th- or 19th-century salon portraits, yet they are never complete. Faces flicker, morph, and sometimes collapse into abstraction. Some images seem convincingly human for a split second, while others unravel into uncanny distortions. The work refuses permanence: no image can ever be repeated or preserved, making the artwork an endless improvisation by the machine.

Memories of Passersby I was exhibited at Sotheby's in 2019, marking a key moment when AI art entered the mainstream art market. Unlike the infamous *Edmond de Belamy* (sold at Christie's in 2018), which was a single GAN-generated print, Klingemann's work insisted on AI as an ongoing process—an algorithmic imagination rather than a static artifact.

Through works like this, Klingemann positioned himself as one of the first truly contemporary "AI artists." His practice highlights not only the strange new aesthetics made possible by neural networks but also the deeper conceptual questions they raise about authorship, originality, and the temporality of art.

From Laboratories to Galleries

By the mid-2010s, AI-generated art was beginning to appear in galleries, festivals, and museums. Exhibitions showcased the strange new aesthetics of machine learning: warped portraits, hallucinatory landscapes, fragmented texts. The "GAN look"—characterized by distortions, glitches, and surreal combinations—became instantly recognizable, much like the glitch aesthetic of earlier digital art.

This was also the period when AI art began to circulate widely online, thanks to open-source tools and artist communities sharing experiments. Unlike earlier periods where access to technology was limited, machine learning tools (though still complex) were becoming more available to independent artists.

Art as Critique of AI

While much of early AI art explored aesthetics, color, and form, some artists turned their attention to the ethical and political dimensions of machine learning. A landmark project in this vein is Trevor Paglen and Kate Crawford's *ImageNet Roulette* (2019), a work that exposed the hidden biases embedded in large-scale AI datasets.

ImageNet Roulette used a subset of ImageNet, one of the most widely used image recognition datasets in AI research. ImageNet contains millions of labeled images, which are used to train algorithms to identify objects, people, and scenes. In the project, users could upload their own image and see how the AI categorized them. The results were often alarming: people were labeled with offensive, stereotypical, or outright absurd categories.

For example, a user might be categorized based on racialized or gendered labels, revealing that the AI's classifications were not neutral reflections of reality but products of historical and cultural biases embedded in the dataset. The project highlighted how training data—carefully curated or otherwise—carries the assumptions, exclusions, and prejudices of its creators and the broader society.

ImageNet Roulette was not only an interactive experience but also a conceptual critique. By turning the AI back on its users, the work made visible the power dynamics hidden inside machine learning systems. It forced audiences to confront questions such as:

- Who decides what is "normal" or "acceptable" in a dataset?
- Whose faces, bodies, and identities are misrepresented or excluded?
- What are the consequences of embedding cultural and racial bias in technologies that increasingly shape daily life?

The work exemplifies a strand of contemporary AI art that does not focus on generating beautiful or uncanny images, but instead interrogates the social and political implications of algorithms. In this sense, the machine becomes not just a tool or medium but a mirror reflecting societal power structures.

Broader Implications for AI and Art

Projects like *ImageNet Roulette* remind us that AI is never neutral. Every dataset, model, and algorithm carries the history, values, and blind spots of its human creators. Artists like Paglen and Crawford make this visible, using art to critique the authority of AI systems and to provoke reflection on their ethical dimensions.

This work also influenced other AI artists and researchers to consider the materiality of data as an artistic and ethical medium. It showed that AI art can be more than aesthetic experimentation—it can serve as cultural critique, exposing inequalities, biases, and hidden infrastructures of machine intelligence.

By foregrounding these questions, contemporary AI artists challenge the audience to see AI not merely as a creative tool but as a cultural and political actor, raising urgent questions about responsibility, representation, and the social impact of technology.

Another example is Hito Steyerl a German artist, filmmaker, and thinker who explores how technology shapes the way we see and understand the world. In her work, she is particularly interested in artificial intelligence and how it affects images, media, and society. Rather than presenting AI as neutral or purely creative, Steyerl focuses on its connection to power, surveillance, and inequality.

In works like *This is the Future* and *Factory of the Sun*, she examines how AI-generated images and algorithms influence what we see and believe. She points out that many AI systems operate as "black boxes," where the decisions behind image creation or selection are hidden from view. This lack of transparency can reinforce existing hierarchies and control the way information circulates.

Steyerl's art asks viewers to think critically about AI: Who controls it? Whose interests does it serve? And how does it shape our collective imagination? By highlighting the social and political implications of AI, she encourages audiences to look beyond the surface of technology and consider the broader consequences of machine-driven creativity.

Why This Period Matters

The 2000s–2010s represent the moment when AI art became recognizably part of contemporary culture. Machine learning gave artists not just new tools but a new conceptual framework: art as training, curating, and collaborating with non-human agents. The questions raised in this decade—about authorship, data, bias, and aesthetics—continue to shape how AI art is made and understood today.

What began with Lovelace's dream of a creative machine, and Cohen's AARON sketching on plotters, had now evolved into a generation of artists working directly with systems that seemed capable of imagination.

Chapter 5 – AI Art Goes Mainstream

By 2018, AI art had moved from research labs and experimental studios into the public eye. Generative algorithms were no longer a niche curiosity for technologists; they had become a central topic in galleries, auctions, and popular media. This period marked a turning point: artificial intelligence was now both a creative medium and a cultural phenomenon, provoking excitement, debate, and controversy about what it means to make art in the age of algorithms.

The Christie's Auction and the Rise of AI Art

One of the pivotal moments that brought AI into mainstream attention was the sale of *Edmond de Belamy*, a GAN-generated portrait created by the Paris-based collective Obvious. The work was sold at Christie's in October 2018 for over $400,000, instantly making headlines around the world.

Edmond de Belamy is the output of a Generative Adversarial Network (GAN)—a machine learning model in which one neural network, the generator, produces images, while another, the discriminator, judges whether they resemble real artworks. Obvious trained the GAN on a dataset of historical portraits, from Renaissance to classical works, teaching the system to mimic patterns in facial structures, costumes, and painting styles.

The resulting portrait is haunting: slightly blurred, with warped facial features and a dreamlike presence. Its

26

fictional subject feels familiar precisely because the algorithm internalized centuries of portraiture. In the bottom corner, instead of a painter's signature, appears the formula that underlies the GAN's process: *min G max D Ex[log D(x)] + Ez[log (1 − D(G(z)))]*—a cryptic but symbolic mark of authorship by the machine itself.

The Christie's sale raised urgent questions of authorship. Was the true creator the algorithm, the Obvious collective who curated the dataset and trained the model, or the wider community of artists whose works provided the training images? This debate marked the beginning of AI art's visibility as a public and cultural issue, not just a technological curiosity.

Théâtre D'opéra Spatial: AI at the Art Fair

If *Edmond de Belamy* brought AI into the auction house, then *Théâtre D'opéra Spatial* brought it into the heart of public debate about the value of art. In 2022, Jason Allen submitted the work—created with the AI system MidJourney—to the Colorado State Fair's fine arts competition. To the surprise of many, the piece won first prize in the digital art category.

The artwork depicts a baroque, operatic scene filled with ornate figures in lavish costumes, set within a richly detailed sci-fi environment. At first glance, it resembled a polished digital painting, but it was, in fact, the product of carefully refined AI prompts. Allen described his role as crafting the prompts and curating the results, comparing it to the artistic process of guiding a brush.

The controversy was immediate. Many artists accused Allen of "cheating," arguing that he had outsourced creativity to a machine. Others defended the entry, suggesting that prompt engineering and curation represent genuine creative acts in their own right. The public uproar—covered widely in the press and on social media—highlighted how AI was no longer confined to research labs or elite galleries. It had arrived in community spaces, competitions, and amateur art circles, forcing broader society to confront its implications.

The Next Rembrandt: Reviving the Old Masters

Another milestone in AI art's public visibility was *The Next Rembrandt* (2016), a project that combined machine learning, data science, and 3D printing to "create" a new painting in the style of Rembrandt. Developed through a collaboration between Microsoft, Delft University of Technology, and several museums, the project analyzed Rembrandt's entire oeuvre—his brushstrokes, use of light, facial proportions, and compositional strategies.

The AI system then generated a new portrait of a fictional man, complete with the textured layering of oil paint achieved through advanced 3D printing. The result was uncanny: it looked like a genuine

Rembrandt, yet it was produced centuries after the artist's death by a machine.

The project sparked both wonder and skepticism. Was this a meaningful act of artistic creation, or merely a technical demonstration? Critics argued that while the system could replicate Rembrandt's style, it lacked the cultural and personal context that gave his paintings their depth. Supporters countered that it revealed how algorithms could act as "art historians," not only analyzing but reanimating the past.

Art, Media, and the Public Debate

Together, *Edmond de Belamy*, *Théâtre D'opéra Spatial*, and *The Next Rembrandt* illustrate how AI art entered the cultural mainstream. Each case became a flashpoint for public discussion, not simply because of the images produced but because of the questions they raised:

- **Authorship**: Who is the artist—the programmer, the machine, or the curator of results?
- **Creativity**: Can a system trained on existing works generate something truly new?
- **Value**: Should AI art compete alongside human-made works in auctions and competitions?
- **Cultural memory**: What does it mean to "resurrect" the style of a dead master through algorithms?

These works made visible the tensions between human creativity and machine automation. More importantly, they signaled that AI had become a public concern, no longer limited to specialized circles of engineers and experimental artists. From the auction house to the county fair, AI art had gone mainstream.

Chapter 6: Text-to-Image Revolution

Following the attention generated by GAN-based works, a new generation of AI tools emerged: text-to-image models, including OpenAI's DALL·E, Midjourney, and Stable Diffusion. These models allowed anyone to generate images simply by typing descriptive prompts. The AI interprets natural language, drawing on vast datasets of images paired with captions to create original compositions.

This technology transformed the creative landscape in several ways:

- **Democratization of Image-Making**: Artists, designers, and hobbyists could produce complex visual works without technical expertise in coding or traditional media. Suddenly, the ability to create high-quality, imaginative visuals was accessible to a broad public.
- **Exploration of New Aesthetics**: Text-to-image models encouraged experimentation with styles, genres, and visual concepts. A single prompt could yield surreal, hybrid images—an architectural structure in the clouds, a futuristic animal, or a portrait in the style of Van Gogh fused with cyberpunk elements.
- **Human–Machine Collaboration**: Artists began to treat AI as a creative partner. By iterating prompts, curating outputs, and refining results, the artist guides the AI without fully controlling

it. The machine's generative unpredictability becomes part of the artistic process.
- **Acceleration of Creative Work**: Tasks that previously took hours or days—illustration, concept art, ideation—could now be achieved in minutes, reshaping both professional practice and amateur experimentation.

While these models opened unprecedented possibilities, they also provoked ethical and legal debates. The datasets used to train these systems often incorporated copyrighted works or biased imagery from the internet, raising questions about consent, originality, and the reproduction of cultural stereotypes.

Cultural Impact and Public Engagement

The mainstreaming of AI art affected culture far beyond the gallery or studio. Social media platforms became flooded with AI-generated images, often shared widely without attribution. The public began to experience AI-generated creativity directly, sparking both fascination and anxiety:

- **Public Perception of AI**: Works like *Edmond de Belamy* and the striking outputs of text-to-image models shaped how society understands AI. They contributed to a perception of machines as capable of creativity—a powerful, almost magical idea.

- **Disruption of Art Markets**: The speed and reproducibility of AI-generated work challenged traditional notions of scarcity and value in the art market. How do collectors value uniqueness when a machine can produce infinite variations?
- **Ethical and Political Debate**: Mainstream AI art made visible questions about labor, bias, and intellectual property. Discussions about who "owns" AI-generated imagery, or whether training datasets exploit human artists, entered public discourse.
- **Integration into Popular Culture**: AI aesthetics have permeated video games, advertising, book covers, fashion, and digital media, blurring the boundaries between professional and amateur production. The visual language of AI is now part of the collective imagination.

Beyond Visual Art

The democratization of AI creativity is not limited to images. Writers, musicians, and performers are now experimenting with text generation (GPT models), music composition (OpenAI's Jukebox, AIVA), and interactive AI performances. AI becomes a collaborator, improvising with human creators and prompting new forms of storytelling, music, and live experiences.

Artists continue to navigate this landscape critically. While some embrace AI for its generative power, others—like Anna Ridler, Mario Klingemann, and Trevor Paglen—use it to interrogate the systems, revealing the biases, histories, and labor hidden behind every model.

Chapter 7: AI and Contemporary Art Today

Artists today use AI in a wide range of ways, turning algorithms into collaborators, tools, and even subjects of critical reflection. Some employ AI to process vast amounts of data—visualizing memory, nature, or cultural archives in ways that exceed human capacity. Others use it as a generative partner, producing variations that spark new ideas or extend their own artistic style. AI can also be embodied in robotics, transforming drawing or performance into a dialogue between human and machine.

The themes explored are equally diverse. Many artists investigate the boundaries between nature and artificiality, reality and imagination, authorship and autonomy. Some focus on the aesthetics of machine "hallucinations," while others emphasize ethical questions of bias, identity, or creativity itself.

The tools range from neural networks and deep learning models to robotics, data visualization software, and custom-built algorithms. What unites these practices is a shared curiosity about how artificial intelligence reshapes not only artistic production but also the way we understand creativity, authorship, and the future of art.

Refik Anadol

Refik Anadol is a Turkish-American artist who has become internationally renowned for his monumental AI-driven installations. Anadol's practice belongs to the field of *generative art*, a form of art where the artist creates the program, rules, and framework, but the machine executes and generates the actual work. This type of AI art requires vast amounts of data to train the system, which then transforms the data into dynamic visual experiences.

One of his most celebrated works, *Melting Memories*, explores the nature of human memory. The piece visualizes brain activity by using data collected from EEG scans. The result is an abstract, dreamlike image world that continuously shifts before the viewer's eyes, creating a poetic bridge between neuroscience and aesthetics.

Another key work, *Machine Hallucinations – Nature Dreams*, draws on 300 million publicly available images of nature. The AI processes these photographs to generate new images—strange hybrids of colors and forms that resemble natural patterns but never replicate them exactly. The work unfolds in real-time on a massive screen, as images melt into one another and dissolve. The viewer is invited to witness not just the final output but also the "hallucinatory" process of the machine itself. Anadol's works thus operate like organic, ever-changing paintings, revealing the ways AI perceives and reimagines our world.

Sofia Crespo

Another artist deeply engaged with nature is Sofia Crespo, an Argentinian-born, Berlin-based artist. Her acclaimed project *Neural Zoo* presents images that resemble the natural world but are, in fact, entirely artificial creations generated by AI. The viewer recognizes the structures as natural, yet they defy classification—these are not real species, but imagined ones.

By training AI on vast datasets of natural imagery, Crespo enables the system to extract patterns and then invent new biological forms. The result is a catalog of fantastical life-forms that feel simultaneously familiar and alien. Through this, Crespo explores biological processes, biodiversity, and even speculative evolution. Her art raises the question: might AI one day help us imagine what evolution could look like millions of years into the future? In Crespo's hands, AI becomes not just a tool of simulation but a collaborator in inventing new worlds and new natures.

Roman Lipski

The Berlin-based, Polish-born painter Roman Lipski offers another perspective on human–AI collaboration. Known for his *Unfinished Series*, Lipski uses AI not to replace his painting but to expand it. After a creative crisis, he turned away from figurative painting and began experimenting with abstraction. To do so, he trained an AI on his own previous artworks, allowing the system to generate countless variations and reinterpretations of his style.

Instead of simply reproducing his paintings, the AI became a dialogue partner, proposing unexpected compositions, color schemes, and motifs. Lipski describes this process as a conversation with AI, one that helps him overcome blocks and discover new artistic directions. His work demonstrates how AI can serve as a muse, sparking inspiration and suggesting fresh pathways in a human artist's practice.

Sougwen Chung

Chinese-Canadian artist Sougwen Chung works at the intersection of drawing, robotics, and AI. In her ongoing project *Drawing Operations*, she collaborates with robotic arms trained on her own hand-drawn gestures. The robots learn her style and then generate their own strokes, which she responds to in real time. Together, human and machine create hybrid works that blur authorship and redefine artistic collaboration.

Chung's art emphasizes process as much as outcome. By engaging in this duet with her robotic counterparts, she explores how machines can extend, echo, and even challenge human creativity. Her installations are not just visual but performative: audiences watch as the dialogue between artist and machine unfolds live, embodying both harmony and tension.

Alexander Reben

Alexander Reben is an American artist, engineer, and roboticist who explores the intersection of human creativity and artificial intelligence. His work often focuses on how machines can not only generate art but also interact with humans in ways that question authorship, agency, and the meaning of creativity.

In his project "Speak Art into Life", Reben uses AI and robotics to create artworks based on verbal input from humans. Visitors speak ideas, stories, or concepts, and the system interprets these prompts to produce drawings or sculptures in real time. The project transforms human imagination into tangible art while highlighting the collaboration between human and machine, showing that AI can extend the creative process rather than replace it.

Another of Reben's projects, "AI Am I?", flips the usual creative process on its head. Instead of a human conceiving an idea and using technology to realize it, this series begins with the AI itself. Reben feeds carefully curated "start texts" into a text-generation AI (GPT), which then produces descriptions of imaginary artworks, along with analyses and contextual commentary. These AI-generated ideas are later brought into the real world by Reben or collaborators, transforming the AI's conceptual output into tangible art.

Across his work, Reben uses AI not just as a tool, but as a conversational partner and collaborator. His projects combine robotics, machine learning, and human interaction to challenge traditional ideas of authorship, highlighting the evolving relationship between human imagination and artificial intelligence in contemporary art.

Conclusion

Together, these artists—Refik Anadol, Sofia Crespo, Roman Lipski, Sougwen Chung, and Alexander Reben—illustrate the diverse ways in which AI is reshaping contemporary art. For Anadol and Crespo, AI is a means of visualizing data and reimagining nature. For Lipski, it is a creative partner that revitalizes his practice. For Chung, it is a collaborator in the act of drawing itself. And for Reben, it is a conceptual tool to probe the philosophical implications of machine-generated creativity.

Chapter 8 – Promptography: Images Without a Camera

It is now possible to create photographs without ever touching a camera. These AI-generated images are often called *promptographs*—pictures born not of lenses and light, but of words. A prompt, a simple text description, replaces the shutter. The term *promptography* was coined in 2023 by the German artist and photographer Boris Eldagsen, whose controversial intervention at the Sony World Photography Awards brought the debate to international attention.

Eldagsen submitted an AI-generated work, *The Electrician*, a black-and-white image reminiscent of staged art photography. When it was awarded first prize in its category, he refused the award. His point was clear: the work was not a photograph but a *promptograph*. Eldagsen wanted to force a debate about the definitions of photography in an age when machines can simulate its look so convincingly. His action made headlines around the world and highlighted the need to distinguish between photography as a record of reality and AI-generated imagery as a product of algorithms.

Annika Nordenskiöld: From Nothing

Swedish artist Annika Nordenskiöld has embraced the medium of promptography in her photobook *From Nothing*. Using AI-generated images, she constructs eerie, surreal scenes in which octopuses, strange figures, and distorted bodies appear in uncanny environments. Nordenskiöld explores not only the creative potential of AI but also its glitches—the strange errors in anatomy and space that machines often produce. These visual oddities are central to her work, inviting viewers to reflect on the limits of machine imagination and the fragility of our trust in images.

By celebrating the weirdness of AI rather than hiding it, Nordenskiöld demonstrates that promptography is not just about realism but about opening up new visual territories. Her work stands as an artistic counterpoint to the commercial drive for flawless AI models in fashion and advertising.

Promptography in Fashion and Magazines

While artists like Nordenskiöld use AI to create uncanny and critical works, the fashion and advertising industries have quickly adopted promptography for more pragmatic purposes. Companies such as Lalaland.ai develop AI-generated fashion models for online retail, offering brands the ability to display clothing on models of different ethnicities, ages, and body types—without hiring anyone.

Magazines have also experimented with AI imagery. Cosmopolitan released an AI-generated cover in 2022, using DALL·E, while other publications have turned to MidJourney for futuristic editorials. These examples bring promptography into the mainstream, raising new questions about the role of human photographers, models, and stylists when digital prompts can replace entire photo shoots.

Documentary and AI Photojournalism

A more controversial field is the use of AI in photojournalism and documentary work. Artists such as Jonas Bendiksen, a Norwegian photographer, experimented early with synthetic images in his project *The Book of Veles* (2021). Bendiksen recreated a photo-essay about a small town in North Macedonia with help of AI-generated visuals, presenting it as if it were traditional reportage. When viewers eventually discovered that none of the photographs were real, the work sparked heated debates about trust, authenticity, and the responsibility of journalism in the age of deepfakes.

Projects like Bendiksen's reveal how promptography challenges one of photography's core functions: its role as evidence. If documentary images can be faked so seamlessly, the credibility of visual media itself comes under question.

Fictional Realities: From Promptography to In-Game Photography

Promptography also shares an affinity with another artistic practice: in-game photography. In video games, players have long used built-in photo modes to "document" digital worlds, landscapes, and events.

Artists such as Duncan Harris (Dead End Thrills) and Justin Berry have built careers on in-game screenshots that resemble high-end photography, despite being captured in fictional environments.

Both promptography and in-game photography operate in the space between reality and fiction. Neither records the external world, yet both borrow the visual language of photography—framing, lighting, and composition—to create convincing images. They challenge the idea that a photograph must be tied to the physical world, expanding it into a spectrum where simulated realities can be "captured" alongside the real.

Conclusion

From Eldagsen's protest at the Sony Awards to Annika Nordenskiöld's surreal explorations in *From Nothing*, from AI models in glossy magazines to Bendiksen's AI-driven documentary experiment, promptography has become both an artistic tool and a cultural battleground. It touches questions of authenticity, labor, representation, and truth itself.

Seen in relation to in-game photography, promptography belongs to a broader cultural shift: photography is no longer bound to the physical world. Today, photographs can be made from data, from text, from pixels of a game engine, or from the glitches of an AI. The challenge is not only to decide what counts as photography but also to rethink what images mean when reality is just one of many possible sources.

Chapter 9 – Art Museums in the Age of AI

In recent years, art museums around the world have begun integrating artificial intelligence in ways that fundamentally transform how visitors engage with art. No longer confined to static exhibitions or traditional audio guides, museums are increasingly using AI to create dynamic, interactive, and personalized experiences that bring artworks and historical figures to life. These innovations allow audiences not only to observe art but also to participate in it, creating a more immersive and meaningful connection with cultural heritage.

One of the most striking developments is the rise of AI-powered interactive portraits. Visitors can now converse with iconic figures or artists from history and art, asking questions and receiving responses generated in real time. Projects that animate the Mona Lisa or other famous works allow these characters to "speak," offering insights into their lives, personalities, and the context in which they were created. Rather than simply viewing a painting behind glass, visitors can engage in a dialogue with it, exploring the story behind the image while feeling as though they are sharing a moment with the historical subject. This approach transforms the museum from a place of passive observation into a participatory space, where audiences actively shape their experience.

One early example is *Dalí Lives* (2019). The Dalí Museum in St. Petersburg, Florida, brought Salvador

Dalí to life through an innovative AI project called *Dalí Lives*. Collaborating with San Francisco ad agency Goodby Silverstein & Partners, the museum fed hundreds of Dalí's interviews, autobiographical writings, and archival footage into an artificial intelligence system. This deepfake technology enables visitors to interact with a lifelike, speaking Dalí, who shares insights about his art, life, and creative process. This pioneering initiative serves as an early example of museums utilizing interactive AI guides to enhance visitor engagement

Some museums are also using AI to provide personalized guidance and storytelling. AI-powered guides analyze visitor preferences, movement through galleries, and even prior knowledge to tailor tours in real time. For example, certain institutions have implemented systems that suggest artworks or provide detailed explanations based on a visitor's expressed interests, creating a journey through the museum that is uniquely theirs. This personalization helps to make large collections more accessible and engaging, giving each visitor the sense that the museum is responding directly to them.

AI is also being applied to art restoration and historical exploration. Advanced machine learning techniques can reveal hidden details of paintings, simulate original colors, and even recreate lost or damaged works. Interactive exhibits allow visitors to explore these discoveries firsthand, seeing layers beneath the surface or learning about the techniques of artists like Leonardo da Vinci in unprecedented depth. In some installations, audiences can virtually step into a three-dimensional reconstruction of a painting, exploring the environment and context in which the artwork was created.

Looking ahead, the possibilities for AI in museums are vast. Future exhibitions may combine holographic displays, real-time motion tracking, and AI-driven narrative systems to create personalized, multi-sensory experiences. Visitors could converse with historical figures, witness AI-generated reinterpretations of famous artworks, or co-create digital pieces that evolve over time. As these technologies develop, museums will become not only repositories of art and history but also active laboratories of imagination, where human and machine creativity intersect.

Ultimately, the integration of AI in museums highlights a broader shift in how we experience culture. By making art interactive, responsive, and adaptive, AI invites audiences to participate in the creative process, blurring the line between observer and creator. In doing so, museums are transforming themselves into spaces where the past is alive, stories are co-authored, and every visitor becomes a participant in the unfolding narrative of art.

Dataland: The World's First AI Art Museum

In 2025, Refik Anadol, a pioneer in AI-driven art, is set to open Dataland, the world's first museum dedicated exclusively to AI art. Located in the heart of Los Angeles at The Grand—a Frank Gehry-designed development—Dataland aims to be a permanent exhibition space for AI-generated art, promoting ethical AI practices and renewable energy usage.

The museum's inaugural exhibition, *Biome Lumina*, will showcase Anadol's "Large Nature Model," a generative AI project trained on environmental data collected using advanced technologies such as LiDAR, photogrammetry, immersive audio, and ultra-high-resolution images taken in 16 unique locations in the rainforest.

Dataland represents a significant step in the integration of AI into the art world, offering a space where human imagination meets machine creativity. It serves as a model for future institutions that seek to explore the intersection of technology and art, providing a platform for artists and audiences to engage with AI in innovative ways.

As museums continue to embrace AI, Dataland stands as a testament to the evolving relationship between art and technology, offering a glimpse into the future of immersive, interactive, and ethically-conscious art experiences.

Chapter 10 – Futures of AI and Art

The rise of artificial intelligence in the art world has sparked a debate that goes far beyond aesthetics. Will AI replace human creativity, or will it expand it? What happens when the cultural record itself is reshaped by algorithms? And how can we safeguard questions of ownership, authenticity, and trust in an age when machines can generate images indistinguishable from "real" artworks?

This chapter explores possible futures for AI and art, through examples that provoke admiration, controversy, and unease.

Expanding or Replacing Creativity?

For many contemporary artists, AI is less a threat than an extension of their practice. Roman Lipski has described his AI collaborator as a "muse," generating new variations on his own work that reignited his creativity. Refik Anadol transforms vast datasets into immersive, hallucinatory experiences, allowing audiences to "see" memory, dreams, and landscapes through machine perception.

But outside the art world, there is genuine concern that AI could replace human creators in commercial fields such as stock photography, advertising design, and illustration. The future of creativity may not be defined by outright replacement but by a more complex redefinition: creativity as a hybrid process, where machines extend the human imagination even as they challenge traditional artistic roles.

Ai-Da: The Humanoid Artist

The British project Ai-Da offers a glimpse into this possible future. Ai-Da is a humanoid robot artist, equipped with cameras in her eyes and robotic arms that allow her to draw and paint. Developed by Oxford researchers and engineers, she is programmed to analyze visual input and produce original artworks. Since her debut in 2019, Ai-Da has exhibited in galleries and even addressed the UK Parliament, sparking global media attention.

Ai-Da's work raises unsettling questions. She can sketch live portraits of visitors, produce abstract paintings, and even write poetry with the help of language models. But is she an artist, or simply a machine performing the motions of artistry? Her creators present her not as a replacement for human creativity, but as a provocation—an embodied thought experiment that asks us to reconsider what creativity means in a world where non-human agents can produce art.

By embodying AI in humanoid form, Ai-Da intensifies our emotional response: it is easier to dismiss a software program as a tool, harder to ignore a robot that looks us in the eye as it sketches our portrait. Ai-Da's presence in the art world illustrates not only technological progress but also the theatrical and cultural dimensions of AI art.

When AI Feeds on Itself

A new problem has emerged as generative AI systems become more widespread: recursive training data. Early models were trained primarily on human-made art, but as AI-generated images flood the internet, new models increasingly train on machine-made images.

This recursive loop risks producing distorted feedback effects—styles becoming exaggerated, forms collapsing into clichés, and originality narrowing. Instead of expanding imagination, AI could end up feeding on its own artifacts, creating a closed ecosystem of synthetic culture divorced from reality.

Some researchers warn of an "AI echo chamber," where datasets filled with synthetic works undermine the diversity and richness of human cultural production. In such a scenario, the question becomes not just *what AI can create* but *what cultural memory we want to preserve*.

Forgery, Authenticity, and Trust

AI's ability to mimic artistic styles also raises urgent questions about forgery and authenticity. If an algorithm can convincingly generate a "new" Van Gogh or Rembrandt, how can museums, collectors, and audiences distinguish authentic works from machine-made fakes?

The 2016 project *The Next Rembrandt*—where a machine generated a new painting in the style of Rembrandt—was presented as a technological experiment, not an attempt at deception. But in less transparent contexts, similar tools could be misused to create fraudulent works.

As AI art becomes more advanced, systems of authentication—signatures, provenance records, blockchain tracking—will become increasingly crucial. Without them, the art market and even cultural heritage institutions risk being undermined by algorithmic forgeries.

Chapter 11: Toward Posthuman Creativity

The future of AI art may lie not in imitation but in moving beyond human frameworks altogether. Artists like Sofia Crespo already use AI to generate fantastical "biologies" that never existed, hinting at aesthetics that are not bound to human perception.

This points to the possibility of posthuman creativity—a cultural space where humans and machines co-create, each contributing strengths the other cannot replicate. But to get there, society must grapple with the ethical, environmental, and epistemic challenges of AI art.

Ownership, copyright, sustainability, authenticity, and cultural memory are all at stake. Projects like Ai-Da show how AI can expand art's horizons, but they also remind us that art is not just about creation; it is about meaning, trust, and responsibility.

The future of art may therefore not be a struggle between human and machine but a negotiation of how both can coexist, creating works that are richer, stranger, and more critical than either could achieve alone.

The intersection of artificial intelligence and art has profoundly transformed how we think about creativity, authorship, and cultural production. From generative installations by Refik Anadol to surreal promptographs by Boris Eldagsen and Annika Nordenskiöld, to humanoid artists like Ai-Da, and from fashion AI models to in-game photography, the landscape of contemporary art demonstrates both the possibilities and challenges of creativity in a technologically mediated world.

Key Insights

1. **AI as collaborator, not just tool** AI has the potential to extend human creativity rather than replace it. Artists like Roman Lipski and Sofia Crespo show that machines can act as sources of inspiration, exploring forms, patterns, and ideas that might remain inaccessible to humans alone. Ai-Da demonstrates the provocative role of humanoid AI in questioning authorship and artistic agency.

2. **Blurring of reality and fiction** Promptography and in-game photography illustrate how AI challenges the traditional function of photography as a record of reality. These works occupy a liminal space, merging human intention and machine interpretation to produce images that are both familiar and alien.

3. **Ethical and societal implications** AI-generated art raises urgent questions about ownership, copyright, sustainability, authenticity, and forgery. Recursive AI training—where new systems learn from AI-generated outputs—further complicates these

concerns, potentially narrowing creative diversity and challenging cultural memory.

4. **Representation and diversity** AI offers both risks and opportunities for representation. While biased datasets may reinforce stereotypes, responsibly curated systems can expand the visual narrative, enabling more inclusive and imaginative depictions in fashion, media, and art.

5. **Posthuman creativity** The rise of AI points toward a posthuman vision of creativity, where humans and machines co-create, producing works beyond the reach of either alone. This challenges conventional notions of originality and emphasizes the hybrid, collaborative nature of contemporary artistic practice.

The Role of Art in Shaping Technological Futures

Art has always played a dual role: reflecting society and imagining alternatives. In the age of AI, this role becomes even more crucial. Artists are not passive consumers of technology—they are critical interlocutors who test boundaries, explore consequences, and provoke societal debate.

Projects such as Ai-Da's humanoid art, and Eldagsen's promptographs demonstrate that art can guide public discourse about technology. These works make visible the promises, limitations, and ethical questions surrounding AI, shaping both aesthetic norms and societal expectations.

Looking Forward: Creativity as a Shared Journey

The next decades of AI and art suggest a future in which the boundaries between human and machine imagination will continue to blur. AI systems may not only imitate human styles but develop their own aesthetic sensibilities, producing works that challenge perception and expand what we consider possible.

At the same time, society must address the ethical, social, and environmental challenges of AI-generated art. Questions of authorship, authenticity, representation, and sustainability will be central to shaping a responsible, inclusive, and imaginative future.

Art in the AI era is a co-evolutionary process. Humans and machines may redefine each other, creating works that are richer, stranger, and more provocative than either could achieve alone. The era of AI invites curiosity, experimentation, and ethical reflection. Creativity is no longer solely human—it is a shared journey.

As we move forward, the challenge is not simply to witness what AI can create, but to engage thoughtfully and collaboratively, shaping technological, cultural, and imaginative futures in ways that reflect our values, curiosity, and vision.

Glossary of Key Terms

AI (Artificial Intelligence)

A branch of computer science focused on creating systems capable of performing tasks that normally require human intelligence, such as learning, reasoning, problem-solving, and creativity.

Algorithm

A set of rules or instructions that a computer follows to solve a problem or perform a task. In AI art, algorithms define how images, text, or music are generated or transformed.

Authenticity

A measure of whether an artwork or image is genuine and can be trusted as what it claims to be. In AI art, authenticity is complicated by machine-generated images and synthetic reproductions of human-made works.

Blockchain (in art)

A digital ledger used to verify ownership and provenance of artworks, often associated with NFTs. It can provide a way to authenticate AI-generated art and prevent forgery.

Deep Learning

A subset of machine learning that uses multi-layered neural networks to analyze and learn from large datasets. Deep learning is commonly used in generative AI, image recognition, and natural language processing.

Diffusion Model

A type of generative AI model that creates images by iteratively refining random noise into a coherent picture, guided by text prompts or training data. Diffusion models are widely used in modern AI art generators.

Dataset

A collection of digital material—such as photographs, paintings, texts, or sounds—used to train AI models. The quality and diversity of datasets significantly affect AI output.

Forgery (in AI art)

The creation of artworks intended to imitate the style of existing artists, potentially deceiving viewers or collectors. AI makes forgery easier, raising questions of ethics and regulation.

GAN (Generative Adversarial Network)

A machine learning framework consisting of two neural networks: a *generator* that produces images and a *discriminator* that evaluates their realism. GANs "compete" until the generator creates convincing outputs.

Machine Hallucination

A term describing the abstract, dreamlike, or unexpected outputs generated by AI systems. It refers to how AI "imagines" based on patterns in training data.

Neural Network

A computational system inspired by the human brain, made up of interconnected nodes ("neurons") that process information and learn patterns from data. Neural networks are the foundation of most AI art systems.

Posthuman Creativity

Artistic practice where creativity emerges not solely from humans but through collaboration with intelligent machines, producing results beyond purely human imagination.

Prompt

A text description or instruction used to guide AI in generating an image, text, or other content. The AI interprets the prompt to produce outputs aligned with the user's intent.

Promptography

A term coined by Boris Eldagsen in 2023 to describe AI-generated photographs created entirely through prompts rather than cameras. It distinguishes AI-generated images from traditional photography.

Recursive Training

A situation where AI models are trained not only on human-created data but also on AI-generated outputs. This can lead to style repetition, narrowing creative diversity, and potential feedback distortions.

Sustainability (in AI art)

Concerns about the environmental impact of training large AI models, which require substantial computational power and energy consumption. Sustainability issues are increasingly relevant as AI-generated art grows.

Training Data

The input material used to teach an AI model patterns and structures. For example, images of historical paintings can be used to train a model to produce new artworks in the same style.

www.ingramcontent.com/pod-product-compliance
Lightning Source LLC
Chambersburg PA
CBHW050021230526
45470CB00003B/1070